WORLD OF

MAMMALS

# TIGERS

**by Peter Murray**

*Content Adviser: Barbara E. Brown, Associate, Mammal Division, The Field Museum, Chicago, IL*

THE CHILD'S WORLD®, CHANHASSEN, MINNESOTA

### TIGERS

Published in the United States of America by The Child's World®
PO Box 326 • Chanhassen, MN 55317-0326 • 800-599-READ • www.childsworld.com

## Acknowledgements:

The Child's World®: Mary Berendes, Publishing Director

Editorial Directions, Inc.: E. Russell Primm, Editorial Director; Pam Rosenberg, Editor;
Judith Shiffer, Assistant Editor; Matt Messbarger, Editorial Assistant; Susan Hindman,
Copy Editor; Emily Dolbear, Proofreader; Judith Frisbie and Olivia Nellums, Fact
Checkers; Tim Griffin/IndexServ, Indexer; Cian Loughlin O'Day, Photo Researcher, Linda
S. Koutris, Photo Editor

The Design Lab: Kathleen Petelinsek, Designer, Production Artist, and Cartographer

## Photos:

Cover/frontispiece: Martin Harvey/Gallo Images/Corbis; half title/CIP: Ralph A.
Clevenger/Corbis.

Interior: Animals Animals/Earth Scenes: 10 (Zigmund Leszczynski), 16 (Lightwave
Photography, Inc.), 20 (Gerard Lacz), 22 (Manoj Shah); Corbis: 5-bottom left and 34
(Pallava Bagla), 12 (Tiziana and Gianni Baldizzone), 18 (Theo Allofs), 21 (Eric and David
Hosking), 31 (Ron Austing/Frank Lane Picture Agency), 32 (Tom Brakefield), 36 (Tim
Davis); Digital Vision: 5-bottom right and 29; Getty Images: 5-top left and 9 (The
Image Bank/Gary Vestal), 5-middle left and 27 (Stone/Schafer and Hill), 25 (Photodisc);
Photodisc: 5-top right and 15.

## Library of Congress Cataloging-in-Publication Data

Murray, Peter, 1952 Sept. 29–
 Tigers / by Peter Murray.
    p. cm. — (The world of mammals)
 Includes index.
 ISBN 1-59296-498-2 (lib. bdg, : alk. paper) 1. Tigers—Juvenile literature. I. Title. II.
World of mammals (Chanhassen, Minn.)
 QL737.C23M87 2005
 599.756—dc22                                      2005000535

# TABLE OF CONTENTS

## Chapter One

# The Devil in the Forest

At the edge of a dense **mangrove swamp,** three nervous men are cutting firewood. One of the men stands watch, staring intently into the sun-dappled forest. The other two men gather bundles of wood. They will use the wood that night to cook rice and lentils for their supper. Just a few dozen meters away, hidden in the shadows, a 150-kilogram (330-pound) female Bengal tiger watches them through large, honey-colored eyes. She is hungry, too—but the tigress does not dream of rice and lentils. She dreams of meat.

This is the Sundarbans, 10,000 square kilometers (3,860 square miles) of mangrove swamp and thick forest on the border of India and Bangladesh. It is one of the last great tiger **habitats.**

Humans are not a favorite food of tigers. The tigress watching the woodcutters would prefer to catch a **chital** or a wild pig. Humans are unpredictable and dangerous. They make strange noises, and they carry weapons. The tigress will not attack unless one of the men wanders

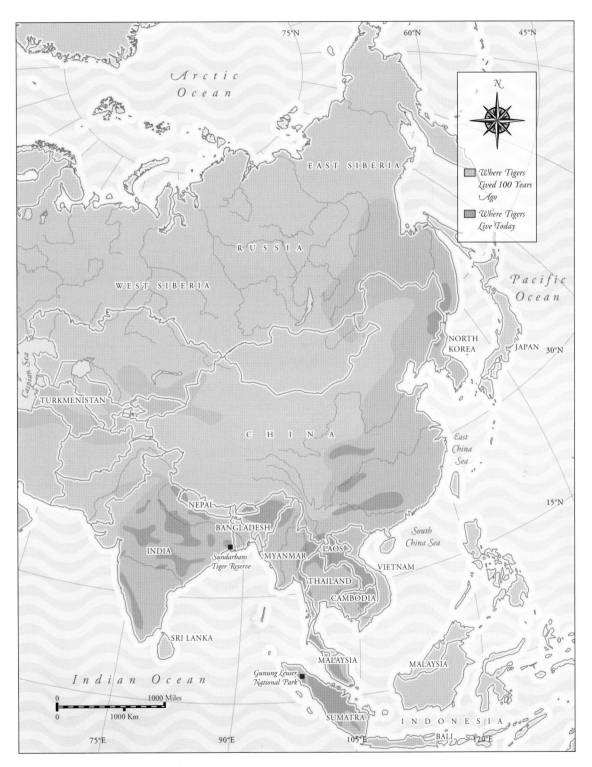

Today, tigers live in a dramatically reduced area.

off into the forest alone. But these three men stay close together. They know that a tiger might be lurking nearby. After a time, the tigress moves off to seek easier **prey.**

Several miles away, a man with a powerful rifle sits in the branches of a tree. He is looking down on a **game** trail, waiting patiently. There are few tigers left in this area. He might wait for days. But he only needs to kill one tiger to support his family for a year.

In the Sundarbans, people are sometimes killed and eaten by tigers. At the same time, **poachers** kill tigers to sell their skin, meat, and bones on the **black market.**

The tiger is a terrifying and powerful beast. But every year, the human population increases, while tigers become harder to find.

Three thousand kilometers (2,000 miles) away, in the forests of eastern Siberia, a pale orange tiger bounds through the snow in pursuit of a young elk. This large male Siberian tiger is nearly double the size of the Bengal tigress in the Sundarbans, and just as hungry. The elk will feed him for several days.

On the island of Sumatra, in Gunung Leuser National Park, a small tigress and her two cubs move silently through the tall grass. The 7,927-square-kilometer (3,061-sq-mi) park is home to many **endangered species,** including Sumatran rhinoceroses, orangutans, clouded leopards, and about 100 Sumatran tigers.

*The Siberian tiger, sometimes called the Amur tiger, is the largest tiger in the world.*

The sound of a gunshot brings the mother tiger to a halt. Hunting is forbidden in the park, but it still goes on. Every year, more tigers are killed by poachers. The tigress turns and moves quickly away from the sound of the gunshot. Her two young cubs follow.

*A tigress and her cub rest in the grass.*

⊕

In the heart of China, where tigers were once common, a male South China tiger searches in vain for a female partner. Only a handful of South China tigers survive in the wild, scattered in isolated pockets of wilderness. This male tiger might survive for a few more years, but he may never find a female of his kind. The South China tiger is all but **extinct** in the wild.

⊕

At the beginning of the twentieth century, Asia was home to more than 100,000 tigers. Tigers ranged from the shores of the Caspian Sea to the tropical island of Bali, and from the snowy forests of Siberia to the southern tip of India.

By the mid-twentieth century, their numbers had been reduced by half. The last tiger on Bali was killed in the 1940s. The tigers of Turkmenistan and other countries near the Caspian Sea have been gone since the 1970s. The Javan tiger has not been seen since the 1980s.

Years of habitat destruction and relentless hunting have reduced the total number of wild tigers to about 4,000. Today, there are more tigers living in cages than there are living in the wild.

*Fishing boats line a riverbank in the Sundarbans Tiger Reserve in Bangladesh.*

## TIGER PROFILE

The Sundarbans is home to the most dangerous tigers on Earth. In most places where tigers live, attacks on people are rare. Tigers are quick learners. They know that humans can be dangerous prey. But in the vast mangrove swamps of the Sundarbans Tiger Reserve, tigers kill and eat people every year. Some years, more than 100 people have been killed by tigers.

Why are the tigers of the Sundarbans so aggressive? Some say it is because the water is salty, making the tigers irritable. Others say that the behavior is learned—mother tigers teach their cubs that humans make good food. The most likely explanation is that in the Sundarbans, men often go into the dense mangrove forests in small groups to gather firewood, collect honey, or fish in the narrow waterways. They tempt the hungry tiger.

In recent years, forest officers from both India and Bangladesh have worked to keep people out of the Sundarbans Tiger Reserve. They have built electric fences to keep tigers away from nearby villages. They have also placed electrified human dummies in the forest. Tigers that attack the dummies get the shock of their lives!

The number of attacks in the Sundarbans has dropped to only a few per year. The people who live in the region are learning to live with the tiger. Perhaps the tigers are learning, too.

**Would You Believe?**
Tigers prefer to attack their prey from the sides and the rear. To reduce tiger attacks, some fishers and honey collectors in the Sundarbans wear human face masks on the backs of their heads.

## Chapter Two

# The Eye of the Tiger

Next time you watch your pet cat sleeping, or stretching, or cleaning itself, or **stalking** a bird, imagine it fifty times heavier. Picture it with claws 12 centimeters (5 inches) long and teeth longer than your thumb. Imagine it with stripes. Then imagine it looking at you as though you were a mouse.

The tiger is a member of the cat family. Tigers are related to lions, cougars, leopards, lynxes, and domestic cats. There are thirty-seven species of wild cat, from the tiny rusty-spotted cat, to the elusive cloud leopard, to the majestic African lion. The tiger is the largest cat species.

Like all cats, tigers are meat eaters, or carnivores. They eat other animals to survive. Dogs, bears, weasels, and mongooses are other examples of carnivores.

The tiger's body is perfectly built for hunting large game. Of all the creatures on Earth, only the human being is more

**Would You Believe?**
The tiger's tiniest relative, the rusty-spotted cat of India and Sri Lanka, weighs less than 1 kilogram (2 lbs)—about one-fourth the size of the average pet cat.

*Tigers are related to lions. They share many characteristics but do not look exactly the same. Male lions have thick manes, but male tigers do not.*

A tiger's huge canine teeth allow it to kill prey with one deadly bite.

deadly. Human beings have intelligence and metal weapons. The tiger's tools include sharp eyes and ears, a flexible body, powerful muscles, quick reactions, enormous teeth, and **retractable** claws.

### CLAWS AND JAWS

Retractable claws are unique to the cat family. A cat extends its razor-sharp claws when it needs them. At other times, they remain **sheathed.** This keeps the claws sharp and ready.

Claws have several uses. They grasp prey as the tiger delivers its killing bite. They are useful for climbing. Adult tigers do not often climb trees, but they can if they want to. Claws are also used for defense against other tigers, for gripping the ground when running and leaping, and for scratching an itch.

Tigers have the largest **canine teeth** of any cat—up to 8 centimeters (3 in) long. A single crushing bite can sever the **spinal cord** of a deer. Their upper and lower teeth work like scissors, shearing through flesh and bone. Their smaller front teeth are useful for stripping away skin and tearing meat from bones. Their rough tongues are used for cleaning the last bits of flesh from the bones of their prey.

## SENSES

There is a saying in tiger country: The tiger will always see you first.

The bright yellow eye of the tiger can detect the slightest movement in bright sunlight or darkest night. Tigers, lions, and other big cats have round pupils,

*Tigers can see about six times better than humans can at night.*

even in bright light. Small cats such as domestic cats, ocelots, and bobcats have vertical, slit-shaped pupils.

A tiger's hearing is its most acute sense. It can tell the difference between the sound of leaves rustling in the wind and a scurrying mouse or a deer making a sudden movement in the brush. In the forest, when it is often impossible to see more than a few feet, hearing is extremely important.

Tigers also have a keen sense of smell. They have openings in the roofs of their mouths that lead to the Jacobson's organ. This organ helps the tiger identify interesting or unusual odors.

Whiskers are long, stiff, highly sensitive hairs that help the tiger feel its way through dense brush. All cats have whiskers. Tiger whiskers grow on their cheeks, **muzzle,** eyebrows, and even on the backs of their front legs.

## COAT AND TAIL

The striped coat of the tiger is its most striking feature. When you see a tiger in a zoo, the black-striped, rusty-orange coat stands out. How could such a brightly colored animal sneak up on wild prey? A tiger's stripes help it blend into its natural surroundings. A tiger in the wild can be almost invisible!

## Would You Believe?

A liger is the **offspring** of a male lion and a female tiger. It has both stripes and spots. The spots come from the lion parent, even though adult lions do not appear to be spotted, and the stripes come from the tiger. Male ligers are the largest cats in the world. They can weigh more than 450 kilograms (990 lbs).

Ligers are sometimes born in zoos and private collections where lions and tigers are raised together and allowed to **mate** with each other. Ligers do not occur in the wild.

Like most wild cats, the tiger has a long, flexible tail. Tiger tails measure more than 1 meter (3 feet) long. Tails help tigers balance when running or climbing. They are also used to communicate with other tigers. A slowly swishing tail held high is a friendly greeting, while a low, twitching tail shows anger. The next time you meet a tiger, remember that.

*A liger (above) is the offspring of a male lion and a female tiger. If a male tiger mates with a female lion, the offspring is called a tigon.*

# Chapter Three

# Making a Living

What does a 250-kilogram tiger eat for dinner? Whatever it can catch!

To survive, a tiger needs 40 to 70 kilograms (90 to 150 lbs) of meat a week. You might think that with those claws and teeth and powerful muscles it would be easy for a tiger to catch its dinner, but in the wild it is not so easy. Nearly all of a tiger's life is spent searching for food.

When hunting, the tiger must stalk to within 15 to 20 meters (49 to 66 ft) of its prey before exploding into action. But wild pigs and deer, the tiger's favorite food, are fast and alert. They will bolt at the slightest sound. A tiger might make dozens of failed attempts before it finally catches something.

Tigers kill by delivering a single bite to the neck. Their powerful jaws and sharp canine teeth

*Wild boar (right) is one of the tiger's favorite foods.*

*A tiger in India delivers a fatal bite to the neck of a chital.*

slice through bone and muscle to cut the spinal cord. If an animal is too large to kill with a bite to the back of the neck, the tiger will crush its throat and hold on until the animal **suffocates.**

A successful hunt means that the tiger will eat well for the next two or three days. The tiger will remain near its kill, eating and sleeping, until all the meat, **entrails,** and small

**Would You Believe?**
A tiger will often cover the remains of its kill with grass and other debris. Then it will return to finish its meal over the next several days.

bones have been devoured. Then the hunt begins again.

**Would You Believe?** A hungry tiger can eat as much as 30 kilograms (66 lbs) of meat in one night.

When food is scarce, tigers will go after smaller game such as peacocks, monkeys, lizards, and even crabs. When they can, they will kill larger animals such as baby elephants or baby rhinoceroses. On the island of Sumatra, tigers have been known to attack orangutans.

Being the biggest and most deadly beast in the forest is no guarantee of a meal. Tigers that are unable to hunt their usual prey will sometimes go after cattle, sheep, and humans. In desperate times, a hungry tiger will even eat grass and berries.

In the wild, tigers that reach adulthood live only ten to fifteen years. One common cause of death is from injuries received while hunting. A tiger with a broken tooth or a fractured leg cannot hunt, and a tiger that cannot hunt will eventually starve to death.

Most cats don't like to get wet, but tigers love the water. In tropical areas,

**Would You Believe?**
Some tigers become man-eaters because they have been injured. Early in the 1900s, on the border of India and Nepal, a single tigress known as the Champawat Man-Eater killed 436 people. She was shot and killed by **naturalist** and hunter Jim Corbett in 1911. When Corbett examined her body, he discovered that both of her canine teeth had been broken off. So humans were the only prey the tigress was able to kill!

where temperatures can reach 50° Celsius (120° Fahrenheit), tigers hit the beach. A refreshing dip in a lake or river helps the tiger stay cool.

Tigers have another reason to stay near water: animals of all kinds are attracted to water. Tigers often lurk nearby, hiding in the underbrush. When a deer or another animal wanders close, the tiger will launch itself from cover and chase its prey right into the water. Tigers have even been known to attack and kill crocodiles.

## FAMILY LIFE

Tigers hunt alone. They do not like to share their food. Each tiger marks its territory by leaving its droppings and

*A Sumatran tiger wades in a river. Unlike most cats, tigers like the water.*

spraying urine and scent on trees. Scratching on trees with their claws is another marking behavior. These signs and odors are a warning to other tigers: *keep out!*

Male tigers have large territories that often overlap the territories of female tigers. Mostly they stay out of each other's way. A mother tiger will defend her cubs if a male approaches. But once her cubs have grown and left her, the tigress becomes more friendly. She sprays trees more often, advertising her presence. Males can tell from the scent she leaves that she is ready to mate. Mating tigers also communicate with roars and other sounds.

After mating, the male tiger leaves. He will not help raise the cubs. In fact, the female tiger will avoid him—male tigers have been known to kill their own offspring.

About four months after mating, in a hidden den, the tigress gives birth, usually to two or three kittens. Tiger kittens are blind and helpless at birth. They weigh only 1 to 2 kilograms (2 to 4 lbs).

Like all **mammals,** tiger babies drink their mother's milk. After four or five weeks, the mother starts to bring them meat. The cubs grow quickly on their meat and milk diet. By the time they are eight weeks old, they have begun to follow

**Would You Believe?**
Though a tigress usually gives birth to a litter of two or three kittens, litters of up to five kittens have been documented.

These Sumatran tiger cubs will be raised by their mother
until they are ready to survive on their own.

their mother on short walks through the forest.

At six months, the cubs are able to follow their mother for greater distances. They no longer need to return to the safety of the den. The tiger cubs get their first hunting lessons. They learn which animals make good prey. They learn to creep up quietly on their chosen victim. They learn to remain perfectly still for long periods of time. Eventually, they learn to kill by delivering a fatal bite to the neck.

It will be many more months before the cubs are able to hunt on their own. They will stay with their mother for up to two years before they have the strength and skills to survive alone.

The first few months after the young tiger leaves its mother is a dangerous time. Each tiger must stake out its own territory, which brings it into contact with other tigers—and with human beings. Inexperienced tigers are lucky to survive their first year. About half of them die from starvation, from wounds received while hunting or fighting, or from being trapped or shot by humans.

Those that do survive will go on to find mates, reproduce, and become an ancestor to future tigers. And so the cycle continues.

## Chapter Four

# Tiger Types

There are five living varieties, or subspecies, of tiger. The Siberian tiger, *Panthera tigris altaica,* is the largest of the tigers. A male Siberian tiger can weigh more than 250 kilograms (550 lbs) and measure 3 meters (10 ft) from its nose to the tip of its tail. Siberian tigers have a long, thick, light-orange coat. About 350 of these magnificent cats live

*Siberian tigers are in danger of becoming extinct. Only about 350 remain in the wild.*

in the remote forests of eastern Siberia. A few may still survive in North Korea and northern China.

Scientists believe that tigers **evolved** in the snowy forests of the north. Siberian tigers are probably very similar to those original tigers. Slowly, over many tens of thousands of years, tigers migrated south and adapted to new, warmer environments.

The most common tiger subspecies is the Bengal tiger, *Panthera tigris tigris*. About 3,500 Bengal tigers live in India, Nepal, and Bangladesh. Bengal tigers are slightly smaller than their Siberian cousins, and their fur is a darker shade of orange.

Farther east, in the forests of Southeast Asia, lives the Indo-Chinese tiger, *Panthera tigris corbetti*. These tigers are slightly smaller than the Bengal tiger—but they are still plenty big: males can weigh up to 200 kilograms (440 lbs). They are dark reddish-orange, with narrow stripes that sometimes break up into short dashes. About 1,000 Indo-Chinese tigers are believed to live in scattered pockets of Thailand, Cambodia, Myanmar, Laos, Vietnam, and Malaysia.

The South China tiger—*Panthera tigris amoyensis*—is the rarest surviving tiger. Fewer than twenty are believed to

**Would You Believe?**
Bengal tigers prey mostly on wild cattle and wild deer.

live in the shrinking patches of forest in southern China. About fifty are living in zoos. Until 1979, this cat was hunted continuously. Today, with only a few South China tigers left in the wild, the Chinese government plans to set aside millions of acres of forest as tiger preserves. They hope to breed and reintroduce tigers to their native habitat.

On the Indonesian island of Sumatra lives the fifth and most unusual tiger subspecies: the Sumatran tiger, *Panthera tigris sumatrae*. Sumatran tigers are the smallest of the tigers, weighing 90 to 120 kilograms (200 to 260 lbs). Their coat is dark reddish-orange with many narrow, closely spaced stripes. They have long facial hair and

*Scientists believe that there are about 1,000 Indo-Chinese tigers still living in the wild.*

**Would You Believe?**
The Sumatran tiger has the darkest coat of all tiger subspecies.

a **ruff** of fur around their neck, giving them a distinctive look. Sumatran tigers are known as excellent swimmers—their large paws have **webbing** between the toes, which helps them move quickly through the water. Confined to seven small parks on the island of Sumatra, these small, graceful tigers may soon follow their close relatives, the Javan and Bali tigers, to extinction.

*This Sumatran tiger, like all tigers, has a distinctive coat of stripes. Did you know that tiger stripes are like fingerprints? No two tigers have exactly the same pattern.*

## Chapter Five

# The Past, the Present, and the Future

For most of human history, tigers have been regarded as dangerous pests. Wherever people and tigers came into contact, two things were sure to happen: tigers killed people, and people killed tigers. It was a contest that the tiger could not hope to win.

A century ago, as many as 100,000 tigers roamed free in Asia. But as human populations grew, the forests were cut down to grow crops. Tigers lost more of their habitat with each passing year.

To make matters worse for the big cats, tiger hunting became a popular sport. In 1951, the Maharaja of Surguja claimed to have personally killed 1,150 tigers. By mid-century, fewer than 50,000 tigers remained.

During the 1950s and 1960s, human populations continued to grow, and the tiger hunting continued. Tens of thousands of tigers were slaughtered. It was not until

the late 1960s that people began to worry about the number of tigers left in the world. The Bengal tiger was listed as an endangered species in 1969.

In 1972, the Indian government conducted a tiger **census.** It estimated that only 1,827 Bengal tigers remained in the wild in India. Later that year, the World Wildlife Fund

*Tigers and other animals are often hunted and killed for their beautiful fur.*

**Would You Believe?**
Some sources estimate that in India poachers kill one tiger every day.

launched Operation Tiger, an international effort to save the last remaining tigers. With money and education from Operation Tiger, India, Nepal, Bangladesh, Indonesia, and other countries set aside land where tigers could live. They passed laws against killing tigers.

In 1973, India launched its own **conservation** program called Project Tiger, eventually setting aside twenty-three tiger reserves. By 1980, the number of tigers in India had increased to more than 3,000.

Still, tigers are in trouble. Each year humans take over more land that was once home to tigers. In China, Japan, and some other Asian countries, tiger parts are used as medicine. Powdered tiger bones are said to cure **rheumatism.** Tiger whiskers are believed to give strength. Pills made from tiger eyes are sold to prevent **convulsions.** Every part of the animal has a medicinal use. One dead tiger can be sold for more than $15,000 on the black market.

Of course, none of these "medicines" has been proven to work. But that doesn't stop people from buying them. And so, throughout the shrinking habitat of the tiger, men with guns lie in wait, hoping to make a quick fortune with a single gunshot.

Will wild tigers still live in the forests of Asia fifty years from now? No one can say for sure. Every year there are more people living on our planet. Every year, there is less room for the tiger to roam.

Today, more tigers live in zoos and in private collections than in the wild. The tiger will not become extinct. But a tiger in a cage is very different from the mysterious and fearsome tiger in the wild. Just imagine a wild tiger padding silently through the jungle sniffing the air. Listening, it flexes its claws, watchfully blinks its great yellow eyes, licks its enormous canine teeth, and waits.

**TIGER PROFILE**
**Estimated Wild Tiger Populations (2004)**
Bengal tiger *(Panthera tigris tigris)* ......................3,100–4,700
Indo-Chinese tiger *(Panthera tigris corbetti)* .........1,200–1,800
Sumatran tiger *(Panthera tigris sumatrae)* .................300–400
Siberian tiger *(Panthera tigris altaica)* .........................300–400
South China tiger *(Panthera tigris amoyensis)* ....fewer than 20
Bali tiger *(Panthera tigris balica)* ............................................ 0
   (extinct since the 1940s)
Caspian tiger *(Panthera tigris virgata)* ..................................... 0
   (extinct since the 1970s)
Javan tiger *(Panthera tigris sondaica)* ..................................... 0
   (extinct since the 1980s)

*A Bengal tiger looks out from a stand of bamboo. Many people are working hard to try to prevent Bengal tigers and other tigers from becoming extinct.*

# Glossary

**black market** (BLAK MAR-kit) the illegal selling or trading of goods

**canine teeth** (KAY-nine TEETH) the large pointed teeth on each side of the jaws of certain animals

**census** (SEN-suhs) an official count of all the members of a group

**chital** (CHI-tuhl) a spotted deer native to India and Sri Lanka; also known as the axis deer

**conservation** (kon-sur-VAY-shun) protecting things that are valuable, especially wildlife and other natural resources

**convulsions** (kuhn-VUHL-shuns) powerful, unexpected movements of a person's muscles

**endangered species** (en-DAYN-jurd SPEE-sheez) a kind of animal or plant that is in danger of dying out

**entrails** (EN-trails) the internal parts of an animal

**evolved** (ih-VOLVED) changed slowly over a long period of time

**extinct** (ek-STINGKT) having no living members of a species remaining

**game** (GAYM) wild animals that are hunted by humans for sport and food

**habitats** (HAB-uh-tats) the places and conditions in which plants and animals live

**mammals** (MAM-uhlz) animals that have backbones, have fur or hair, and drink their mother's milk

**mangrove swamp** (MAN-grohv SWAHMP) coastal forested wetlands found in tropical and subtropical climates

**mate** (MAYT) the act of a male and female animal coming together to produce offspring

**muzzle** (MUHZ-uhl) the nose, mouth, and jaw of an animal

**naturalist** (NACH-ur-uhl-ist) a person who studies animals and plants

**offspring** (OFF-spring) the young of an animal

**poachers** (POH-churs) people who hunt animals illegally

**prey** (PRAY) animals that are hunted down and eaten by other animals

**retractable** (re-TRAK-tuh-buhl) something that can be drawn or pulled back in is retractable

**rheumatism** (ROO-muh-ti-zuhm) a disease that produces pain in the muscles and joints

**ruff** (RUFF) fur or feathers that resemble a collar around the neck of an animal

**sheathed** (SHEETHD) to be pulled back into a covering

**spinal cord** (SPY-nuhl KORD) a thick bundle of nerve tissue that runs through the backbone

**stalking** (STAW-king) the act of hunting in a secret, silent way

**suffocates** (SUF-uh-kates) dies from not getting enough oxygen

**webbing** (WEB-ing) tissue or membrane that connects the fingers or toes of certain animals

# For More Information

## Watch It

*Hidden World of the Bengal Tiger,* DVD (Washington, DC: National Geographic, 2004)

*Land of the Tiger,* DVD (Washington, DC: National Geographic, 1993)

*Tigers of the Snow,* DVD (Washington, DC: National Geographic, 2004)

## Read It

Bartolotti, Dan. *Tiger Rescue: Changing the Future for Endangered Wildlife.* Buffalo, N.Y.: Firefly Books, 2003.

Montgomery, Sy, and Eleanor Briggs. *The Man-Eating Tigers of Sundarbans.* Boston: Houghton-Mifflin, 2001.

Osborne, Mary Pope. *Tigers at Twilight.* New York: Random House, 1999.

Seidensticker, John. *Tigers.* Stillwater, Minn.: Voyageur Press, 1996.

Swain, Gwenyth, and John F. McGee (illustrator). *Tigers.* Chanhassen, Minn.: Northword Press, 2002.

## Look It Up

Visit our home page for lots of links about tigers:
*http://www.childsworld.com/links*

Note to Parents, Teachers, and Librarians: We routinely verify our Web links to make sure they are safe, active sites—so encourage your readers to check them out!

# The Animal Kingdom
# Where Do Tigers Fit In?

**Kingdom:** Animal

**Phylum:** Chordates (animals with backbones)

**Class:** Mammalia (animals that feed their young milk)

**Order:** Carnivora (meat-eating mammals)

**Family:** Felidae (the cat family)

**Genus:** *Panthera* (the big cats)

**Species:** *tigris*

# Index

## About the Author
Peter Murray has written more than 80 children's books on science, nature, history, and other topics. An animal lover, Pete lives in Golden Valley, Minnesota, in a house with one woman, two poodles, several dozen spiders, thousands of microscopic dust mites, and an occasional mouse.